Understanding Sasquatch Behavior

How to Find Bigfoot

by Dave Gibson

Copyright

Other books

by Dave Gibson:

Living Among Sasquatch: A Primer (nonfiction)

A chronicle of Pamela's and my experiences in learning that not only were Sasquatch real, but that we were living among them in our cabin in the woods.

Living Among Little People: A Guide for Sasquatch (almost all fiction)

Generally follows the same story as *Living Among Sasquatch* but told from our Sasquatch's perspective. It is a tongue-in-cheek narrative where our Sasquatch misinterprets just about everything he observes us doing, with a good dose of action and suspense.

Weak in Body, Strong in Mind and Spirit (completely made up, except the people and places are real)

This book is a real hoot. That's probably all I can say about it. This came from my alleged brain, which should not come as a surprise anyone who knows me.

Dedication

This book is dedicated yet again to my loving wife, research partner, and one of the best 'Squatchers I know, Pamela. Who also has a good heart.

To my daughter, Rebecca, my sister Kathleen, and my dozens of cousins everywhere who know I'm a bit whacked but talk to me anyway, at least on Facebook. And a few admit that we're related.

To the Forest People, especially Pamela's special young hairy friend Madu, who befriended us and didn't eat our dogs. Or us.

To Native Americans for documenting their stories of Sasquatch, but especially to the Iroquois who set Pamela and I on the right path to understanding the Keepers of the Forest.

To Shirley McDaniel, a very wonderful artist who, like me, may have a spiritual connection to Sasquatch and draws what she envisions. It is nice to know that I am not alone.

Table of Contents

Foreword by the Author:

Bear with me a bit here. I'll explain.

I have had several careers over my 67 years on this planet. Like the weather in Vermont, if you don't like it, wait a minute.

My first summer job after high school was as a janitor cleaning up the school I had just graduated from cleaning up the mess my classmates and I made all year. But then it was off to college in the fall.

After my freshman year, my college said that since I had an aversion to going to class, I should not return.

I then became a machinist apprentice at General Electric. I loved it! Precision machining is a hoot! I excelled and then became a toolmaker apprentice, the epitome of machine work. But sadly, I couldn't live on the pittance the company paid apprentices, so I left for greener pastures.

My next job was in commission retail sales, selling appliances for the W.T. Grant Company. I worked hard and did well, so well that I was soon promoted to department manager of the appliance and furniture departments at a small Grant's store. There, I reorganized the displays and balanced the inventory to maximize sales. My young wife and I bought a nice mobile home and moved out of our apartment.

Seeking yet better pay to support my young family, I was hired to manage a furniture and appliance outlet for a small local chain. I soon started outselling the main store, much to the annoyance of the salesmen there. Warehouse sales was the future, I figured. I was right, since the internet hadn't been invented yet.

Then it was on to commission automobile sales and even more pay. Again, I worked hard and did well and was promoted to new car and truck manager. I ordered attractive vehicles, balanced our inventory, and properly appraised trade-ins. I sold our mobile home and bought a house. I was 25 years old.

But something didn't feel right about my life. I was working too many hours, including evenings and weekends. I wasn't living. I was missing the normal life of a young man with a family.

I announced to my wife that I intended to return to college, much to her dismay. I hied myself to a local community college and enrolled in data processing, as it was called then. I worked selling appliances and "brown goods" (TVs and stereos) for Montgomery Ward part time while I took college courses full time. In my last semester, at my manager's request, I also worked full time. It was tiring, but I graduated with a 3.98 GPA. That crummy B in tennis messed up my perfect GPA. I was 32.

I took a job as a Cobol programmer, but was quickly promoted to Cobol Department Manager and lead systems designer of financial and human resource systems for government agencies. Soon, I was promoted to vice-president. I made a million bucks for the company in my first year as VP. Sadly, it was two million in debt and the company folded. I was 38.

I went off on my own, tired of working for others, and continued developing software. I also opened a retail computer store since I knew both sales, retail, and computers so well. Even though we were 50 miles from the capital district of Albany in a little town in a rural county, within a couple of years we were #10 in the top twenty-five largest computer dealers' list of the Capital District Business Review. I soon had a dozen employees and was doing over a million dollars in sales annually. This was in a "city" of 15,000 in a rural county of 50,000. Honesty and hard work was rewarded. I bought a very nice one hundred year old home in a nearby town and became a well known businessman, participating in chamber of commerce activities and local charities.

I ran my business my way. I didn't follow the methods of others. Prospective new hires would often be taken aback by my unique interviews and work policies. For example, I explained that we had no sick days. If you're sick, stay home and I'll pay you. Don't come to work and infect everyone else, especially me. Never call in sick because you want a day off. That is dishonest and I'll fire you in a heartbeat. Call and tell me you need a day off and I'll give it to you and pay you, no questions asked. If you make a mistake, tell me so we can figure out how to fix it. I never fired anyone for making a mistake. We all make mistakes. Hide a mistake and you're fired for being dishonest.

I decided our downtown needed to market itself better and I, along with a handful of like minded business people, founded a BID, or Business Improvement District.

The local YMCA moved out of downtown to a remote location and our kids couldn't get there without transportation, so Pamela and I founded a Boys & Girls Club. This is a very wonderful organization that welcomes all kids and gives them a safe place to gather after school. Support your local B&GC. If you don't have one, consider starting one.

During this time, the internet caught on, and along with it, social media. Perhaps the first were message boards where folks with similar interests and hobbies congregated to discuss (and argue) various topics about their avocation. Being an avid sailor, I frequented several sailing boards. I posted about cruising in the Caribbean and what I learned. Most cruisers disliked what were called boat boys, who were men who motored around anchorages selling everything from fruit and vegetables, to fresh baked bread and tee shirts. They were considered a nuisance. I didn't see it that way, I wrote, and I thought they were entrepreneurs who saw a need and filled it. I was contacted by the editor of the magazine who hosted this message board and asked if he could publish it. He did, and I got a nice little check in return. So began my part time career as a writer of magazine articles.

The recession of 2008 hit and my business of twenty years had to close. A record 6,000 businesses shut down that year, a record number not broken until 2017, We moved to Stamford,

Connecticut and I worked for a sailing company and Pamela was a vet tech for a veterinarian. I was 59.

Then I retired. It was time. I was now 60. It was now or never. How many folks do you know who worked until the last minute, retired, and then promptly died? I had things to do besides work and write magazine articles. It was time to live.

Pamela and I bought an old trawler. It sat "on the hard" for over 20 years, uncovered and neglected, but it was within our price range. We spent a year getting it in running order. We named it Drift Away after the Dobie Gray song. The lyrics, in part...

> Oh, give me the beat boys and free my soul
> I wanna get lost in your rock and roll and drift away
> Give me the beat boys and free my soul
> I wanna get lost in your rock and roll and drift away

Pamela and I cruised down the eastern seaboard from Stamford, to Albany New York, and then leisurely down to below Jacksonville Florida on Drift Away. While doing so, I wrote a popular blog about our adventures. You can sample it here...

https://trawlerdriftaway.blogspot.com/

We eventually sold Drift Away and bought ten acres of land in a tiny town in the lower foothills of the Adirondack Mountains of upstate New York. And that finally brings us around to Sasquatch, which is the topic of this booklet.

Why am I writing about my varied career history? I think it helps to understand me as a person, and as an author, and why I write books like this one. I've never been one to follow the crowd, only to make the same mistakes they did. Like Ol' Blue Eyes sang, I did it my way. I can make my own mistakes, thank you.

I have character traits that I am proud of. Hard work and honesty, mainly, was pounded into me by my grandma who was of Irish descent. "Be the job big or small, do it well or not at all" my grandma taught me, as she was taught. That simple phrase did me well my entire life, and I was recognized for it by each of my bosses who promoted me. I made them look good. I was good for business. Customers liked being treated with honesty and respect. In truth, I was not smarter than anyone else, just hard working. Even today, a couple of other retired guys and I started a little business to keep busy. The name, and our motto?

The Old Goat Fence, Deck, and Yard Work Company: If we ain't in the hospital, we show up!

In life, showing up is important.

So what is the purpose and point of all this rambling? Work hard at your Sasquatch research. Be honest about anything you find or learn. Be open minded. Consider thinking outside of the box. Don't merely accept what is considered mainstream thinking. Think for yourself. Don't accept the claims of others as gospel truth. Observe. Form theories and then try to confirm them, if possible. Be pragmatic. Whatever works. Do not be trapped by conventional thinking. Sasquatch are not apes. Do not apply ape thinking to your research.

That work history, my friend, is exactly how I approached my discovery that Sasquatch were real, and that they were all around us. I took on Sasquatch the exact same way I tackled being a machinist/toolmaker, a retail salesman, a second attempt at college, my own business, our voyage down the east coast, writing magazine articles and blogs, and finally writing about Sasquatch. Hard work, honesty, and thinking outside of the box.

So what of the other Sasquatch researchers and fans who think differently and approach Sasquatch from a whole other angle? Most are sincere, some are not. Some are on the right track, some are not. Some in the Sasquatch community just seem to be seeking attention.

Truly, this is not me. I've been there, done that. I have been the president of more organizations than I can shake a stick at. TV, newspaper, and radio interviews were my thing for a time. I don't need or want attention. The handful of podcasts that I've done were not to attract attention to me, but rather to the truth.

Some indeed do seek fortune though. Well, suffice to say that despite the fact that my books are selling well for a topic about a creature that only 10% or so of the population think might exist, the royalties are certainly not enough to call a fortune. Maybe enough to buy a junk used car. The hourly rate is horrible. Write a good romance novel and you might make a tidy sum, but not books about cryptids.

Why do I write? Well, I love to write, number one, ever since I was a child. After having the wind taken out of my sails (see the clever sailing reference there?) by my tenth grade English teacher who said I couldn't write, I'd writen articles for boating magazines for a couple of decades, and then wrote the blog about cruising on our trawler Drift Away, and then yet another blog about building an off-grid home in the Adirondacks. To my surprise, this last blog became peppered with reports of Sasquatch. You can find that one in the following link.

http://bleeckermountainlife.blogspot.com/

Search the blog for "Bigfoot" and "Sasquatch" and you can follow our learning process as it happened to us.

So writing isn't new to me. Sasquatch is though. My first book *Living Among Sasquatch: A Primer* documented our learning curve regarding Sasquatch. But the more I learned, the more it seemed I didn't know. But also the more I became slowly convinced that many researchers were going about things the wrong way, and either not getting any results at all, or were so desperate to get results that they became victims of misinterpreting evidence and even pareidolia, seeing imaginary Sasquatch faces in the shadows that they would highlight with red circles as proof they were having encounters.

This booklet describes typical Sasquatch behavior, and how to use that knowledge to improve your odds of collecting genuine evidence or perhaps even having close encounters of your own.

Introduction:

This is a nonfiction book. But it got me thinking about the definition of nonfiction versus fiction.

A work of fiction is a fabrication. Something completely made-up. A product of the author's imagination. My novels are fiction, although there is an element of truth in them. Both novels contain real people and real places, but the plot and the scenes I created are imaginary.

nonfiction is a journal of sorts. A recording and reporting of facts. It is permissible to recreate some elements, such as dialogue, but a work of nonfiction must portray events and people accurately to be taken as a serious work. My first book is nonfiction and describes my wife Pamela's and my encounters with Sasquatch.

But what is this one? Certainly, it is nonfiction in that it relates my understanding of Sasquatch behavior and the most effective way for one to interact with these amazing beings. I am part of a small minority, however. I have yet to encounter others with beliefs regarding Sasquatch that match mine, with only a few rare exceptions. But what if I'm proven wrong someday? Is it still a work of nonfiction? If I'm found to be right, does that mean that everyone else is wrong and their books now become fiction?

Should I refer to this booklet as an op-ed piece like the editorials in your daily newspaper, opinions based on facts? Or, as we referred to similar writings in the computer world, a white paper? An authoritative treatise based on the writer's findings? Since a white paper isn't an option when publishing a book, I went with nonfiction, but white paper is more accurate.

I guess I'll just let the reader decide. Take it for what it is. To me, it is nonfiction because it describes Sasquatch behavior as accurately and I can portray it based on our habituation experiences. Pamela and I spent three years living among them, except winters when we hightailed it out of the mountains and headed to warmer climes. The one year we stayed until January, our Sasquatch buddy had already beat big feet to parts unknown. We saw no signs of him. But we learned a great deal during the times he was about, which is presented in this book.

This is for you, buddy. Thanks.

Chapter 1: What is Sasquatch?

This topic is one that sticks in my craw. Bear with me.

The majority of Sasquatch aficionados consider Sasquatch to be a North American gorilla-like ape of some sort. They refer to Sasquatch as animals, and like all big wild animals, they should be feared. Why most think this way, I am not sure. Perhaps it is because they are covered in long hair and live in the forest. But since so little is known about them, calling them an animal is jumping to conclusions, in my opinion. Sasquatch is no more an animal than we are.

When I first started researching Sasquatch, I thought of them as apes too because that's what everyone claimed. That's all I read in books and online. That is what my initial research turned up. But as our own interactions with our local Sasquatch grew more frequent, I realized they were much too intelligent and human acting to be merely a gorilla-like ape, even compared to Koko, the kitten loving gorilla who communicates with humans using sign language.

It was when I started researching Native American beliefs in Sasquatch that it all started to make sense to me. The five nations of the Iroquois are the Mohawk, Oneida, Onondaga, Cayuga, and Seneca. Later, the Tuscarora joined the confederation.

The Mohawks were referred to as the Keepers of the Eastern Door. The Oneida, the People of the Standing Stone (I'll explain shortly). Onondaga, Keepers of the Central Fire. Cayuga, the People of the Great Swamp. The Seneca, Keepers of the Western Door.

The name Adirondack, as in the Adirondack Mountains of upstate New York, is derived from the Iroquois word "Ratirontak", meaning "land of the bark eaters", or "they eat trees". It was said (assumed?) to be a derogatory term used to describe the

Algonquins who would resort to eating certain parts of trees in winter when food was scarce. Maybe, maybe not. Perhaps they were referring to Sasquatch.

Sasquatch were called "the Keepers of the Forest" by the Iroquois. Now ponder that a bit. Sasquatch were accorded the same status as the various tribes of the Iroquois. The Iroquois often said that Sasquatch were another tribe of people. One account I read said that they even traded with Sasquatch. The Iroquois honor all things in nature, but never referred to, say, bear as another tribe. Only Sasquatch

The Iroquois referred to Sasquatch as "stone giants", "stone coats", or "stone clads". Sasquatch were said to roll in stone dust to ward off arrows and other weapons. My hunch, after living in the Adirondacks, is it is to ward off mosquitoes and black flies.

So... stone giants or stone coats... standing stone? Is there an actual connection to Sasquatch? What we know from Iroquois legend, stone giants and stone coats most certainly refer to Sasquatch. They were said to stand twice as tall as a human and have stone armor that repelled arrows and other weapons. But what of standing stone?

There are several Iroquois legends regarding the term standing stone. One is that whenever an Oneida village would move, a "standing stone" would direct and guide them to a new location. A Sasquatch covered in stone dust? Perhaps. Just something interesting to ponder as I connect dots here.

No one can state with certainty exactly what Sasquatch are. That would require at least a body to ascertain it. So we are left to guess. Some guesses are educated, and some are not. Some are wild guesses. Some are to sell books of scary mountain monsters who would kidnap your women. And yes, some are crazy, as in Sasquatch are extraterrestrial and arrive here on UFOs and travel through portals to other times and dimensions. Sigh.

Chapter 2: Mindspeak; is it real?

I am not a "woo person". I don't believe cloaking is real, nor portals to other dimensions or time. I have never seen evidence of such a thing. Of course, that is the idea of cloaking and portals, I suppose. There is, however, some evidence of mindspeak, or mental telepathy.

Many have had a sense that something terrible had occurred only to get a dreaded phone call that someone close had died. Or a person who got a sense of warning not to do something, such as to board an airplane which later crashes. My father-in-law had a meeting at the World Trade Center one morning but something deep inside told him not to go, so he didn't. It was September 11, 2001.

Is this mindspeak? Intuition? Luck? Or just plain coincidence?

It was Sigmund Freud's opinion that we have three minds, a conscious, preconscious, and an unconscious. Our conscious mind is how we think, process data, and form opinions of which we are aware. It works when we are awake. Our preconscious is where we store often needed information, such as telephone numbers, names, and addresses. Our unconscious mind always works in the background, twenty-four hours a day, and influences behavior, feelings, and judgment.

I learned when tackling complex computer problems to set everything aside and do something else. Take a shower, go fishing, doodle... anything but concentrating on the problem. Almost always, the problem was solved by my unconscious or preconscious brain. Have you ever struggled to remember someone's name and finally gave up, to only have it pop into your head while you were doing something totally unrelated? That is your unconscious or preconscious brain at work.

I have written about the process of writing my novels. Trust me, I did not write them. Not the conscious me sitting at my laptop and concocting a story about Sasquatch life and culture. I did not have the ability to do so and had writer's block at 13,000 words into my first novel. I was at a standstill. It was only when one of my goats ate my outline (there's a new excuse for your children to explain where their homework went) and I just typed mindlessly that a story magically unfolded before me, 80,000 words worth per novel. Was this my unconscious brain working? Or was my novel being dictated by someone else? Was I channeling someone? So as a gag, I added "by Madukarahat, as told to Dave Gibson" to the title, Madukarahat being my main Sasquatch character.

HA HA, good one!

A few months ago, early in the morning, I was sound asleep. "HONOBIA" was yelled at me, waking me up with a start. I sat up and looked around. Pamela was working and I was alone. What the heck is a honobia? I never heard of a honobia. Well, I was going to go back to sleep, but since the word honobia was even spelled for me, I got up and googled it.

Go ahead, google it. I'll wait.
>
>
>
>
>
>

Strange, eh? I have no idea what that means, being awakened by HONOBIA. I had never heard of it before. Not in the books I've read, and not in any Facebook groups.

So... a family in Honobia Oklahoma started experiencing Sasquatch around their remote home, not too unlike Pamela and me. After a brief period of uncertainty, we quickly accepted and enjoyed our Sasquatch's company. The Honobia family did not and started shooting, claiming to have killed one.

Was I told to write this book by our Sasquatch who wanted me to explain to you what Sasquatch really are and how they live? Using mindspeak? As if that's a real thing?

Sure, I used mindspeak in my novels, but only to enable Sasquatch and humans to communicate, using thoughts instead of words. In my novels, mindspeak also works over long distances. It was to facilitate communication between two different species, a writer's trick. But now Honobia?

Just one more thing to ponder, could mindspeak actually be a real thing? We humans have been trying to prove mental telepathy is real for over a hundred years, at least. Where did the idea come from? An interesting thought to mull over. Honobia.

I'd been trying to decide what to write about next, my fourth book, after finishing my third, a novel called *Weak in Body, Strong in Mind and Spirit*. It would be another novel, I figured, since I discovered that I love writing fiction. Most of my writing had been nonfiction, as in my blogs, many magazine articles, and first book *Living Among Sasquatch: A Primer.* In nonfiction, I am merely researching, documenting, and reporting facts. But in fiction, if I can imagine it, I can MAKE it happen. I can make Skunk Apes fly or vanish, kidnapped by balls of light called sprites! What a hoot! However, I ultimately decided my next novel will have to wait and be my fifth or sixth book and would have to be another time. The little book you're holding needed to be written first.

Honobia is a town in southeastern Oklahoma. Much has been written of the "siege at Honobia", a series of events that happened in 2000.

A family hunted deer on their property. The family had planted Austrian Snow Peas on their land, a favorite of deer. Deer were attracted to their property, and Sasquatch were attracted by the deer. Sasquatch, being curious and inquisitive by nature, were also interested in this family and no doubt observed their activities, as our Sasquatch did with Pamela and I. The Honobia Sasquatch scared the family by knocking on their windows and walls, as Sasquatch are prone to do, to watch the family's reactions.

To a Sasquatch, it seems that watching people through their windows is akin to Sasquatch TV for them. They did the same to us in our little cabin deep in the woods, but we enjoyed knowing our Sasquatch was about and watching us. There might be a knock on a window, or a slap on the side of the house... our Sasquatch is here, we'd smile!

The Honobia Sasquatch also helped themselves to deer meat in a freezer in an open shed. Remember, Sasquatch share. Which means you share. Sharing food is what they do, so it is what you do.

The men in the Honobia family spotlighted their woods at night and started shooting at Sasquatch, they claimed. This apparently was very annoying to the Sasquatch and they responded by screaming and throwing rocks. The men later claimed they killed a Sasquatch. The other Sasquatch retrieved the body and carried it away and then never returned. The family was lucky. They wouldn't have liked it if the Sasquatch decided to get revenge.

The "siege at Honobia" was a situation where understanding Sasquatch behavior might have saved the affected family much angst and maybe would have saved a Sasquatch life, if they indeed shot one. Misunderstanding Sasquatch possibly got a Sasquatch killed and perhaps could have endangered members of the family as well. If this account is true, and because it also could have gone badly for the human family as well, I was compelled to write this booklet.

Knowing what I know now, the family's actions were completely the wrong things to do. In this little book, I will later explain why.

So am I being told to write about Honobia by our Sasquatch who have found a voice in me somehow? Or am I nuts, and somehow I stumbled across Honobia somewhere and the word just popped into my head? I have no idea. But I do know I am moving mindspeak from the woo category to the "it might be possible" column.

What I suspect is that Pamela's and my habituation experiences, while not unique, are unusual in the Sasquatch community and our reactions are not mainstream thinking at all. Most believe Sasquatch are terrible monsters, even though there is not one documented, verifiable instance of a Sasquatch killing or otherwise attacking a human. Only legends and scary campfire stories that float around the internet.

In our case, we quickly learned that not only wasn't our Sasquatch a threat to us and our pets, and certainly no dangerous Adirondack Mountain Gorilla-like ape, but are very intelligent beings that watched over us and our pets. We not only grew accustomed to our Sasquatch, but became very fond of him (or her, but in the interest of brevity, him). And he became fond of us. We interacted with each other regularly and enjoyed each others company.

For instance, I was often outside the cabin on moonless nights in pitch blackness, setting up my camera to take star photos. He would sometimes run behind me to let me know he was there, and I would smile and keep on setting up. Our Sas was here to watch, I'd think. I didn't panic. I knew he was curious as to what I was doing.

Typically, those who find that they have Sasquatch about are frightened (as we kind of were at first) and get out the guns. I can't fault them for it since most people are afraid of Sasquatch. Fearing for their lives is what they are told in books, TV, and social media. As my imaginary Sasquatch say in my novels "they (meaning us) hate what they don't understand". And now you can see where I'm going with this. My job is to help you understand

Sasquatch behavior, to understand that while you certainly should be cautious, you should not be afraid. And you should definitely not get out the guns and start shooting. They hate that.

Chapter 3: Why So Many Reports of Aggression?

That's the first question people ask when I talk or write about the People of the Forest. But first, let me explain about experts if you're somewhat new to the Sasquatch community. There aren't any. There are some very seasoned researchers and trained scientists that I think are on the right track, my favorite being Dr. Jeff Meldrum who has analyzed Sasquatch in his book *Sasquatch: Legend Meets Science*. But experts? None, me included. But what follows is my honest opinions of their behavior based on habituating with Sasquatch for an extended period of time.

There are many researchers who claim aggressive behavior by Sasquatch. The tales I seriously question are reported bluff charges. A bluff charge is ape behavior, and also exhibited by some animals. Most researchers believe Sasquatch to be some species of North American Ape, and so some claim being bluff charged. My guess is that they do so to impress friends and it never actually happened. I'm not impressed. Sasquatch do not bluff charge based on Pamela's and my own experiences, and they had plenty of opportunities to do so during our time in the mountains. Apes do bluff charge, of course, as well as elephants, rhinoceroses, and water buffaloes. In North America, a mother bear with cubs on rare occasion might bluff charge to chase you off should you get too close.

If an African Mountain Gorilla, say, feels someone is a threat to his family who are munching on leaves nearby, he will aggressively charge to chase the person off. No surprise there. If you're a gorilla.

Now consider a Sasquatch. I am firmly convinced they are a people not too unlike us. Very big and hairy, for sure, but a people. If you were berry picking in the woods with your family and a total stranger half your size appeared, what would you do? You might introduce yourself and in a friendly way ask what he's doing there. But if you perceived him as a possible threat because he was carrying a rifle in one hand and a knife in the other, you would most likely position yourself between your family and the threat. But would you bluff charge? Run at this person while screaming and waving your arms about? I seriously doubt it. You might get killed, and then your family would be exposed to danger. You would do the safe thing and take your family and leave, while keeping a wary eye on the threat.

An adult Sasquatch would be no different. His or her foremost job is to protect family. The family would stay hidden while the adults watched the intruder. If a perceived threat approached too close, the adult will warn by yelling or screaming, the Sasquatch equivalent of "Hey! Get out of here! Scram!" Perhaps toss a few rocks or sticks in your direction, which is understood in any language as not welcoming. But charge? No. That is how you get killed, and then your family is truly exposed to danger.

Now, all that being said, I need to add that I am open to the idea that there may very well be more than one cryptid that we lump into one species and call Sasquatch, such as the possible existence of Skunk Apes (different from Sasquatch) and Dog Men, but since my experiences are all with Sasquatch, that is what this book will address. Exercise caution nonetheless until you are sure what you are dealing with. Don't be reckless. And don't panic.

Typical Sasquatch behavior when you are entering an area that you shouldn't is for them to toss small rocks in your direction to get your attention. This seems to be universal behavior with Sasquatch everywhere and happened to two researchers from Ohio out 'Squatchin' with Pamela, and once even to Pamela herself. If this happens, you should leave, because what happens next is that the rocks or sticks get bigger and bigger, and closer and closer. Too close, and if you make any perceived threatening moves towards the Sasquatch or his family, you may get clobbered by a rock or club.

Well, isn't this aggressive behavior, you're thinking? What's wrong with you, Dave? You're not making any sense and contradicting yourself. No, not on purpose anyway. This is defensive behavior, not aggressive, and you should heed the warnings. Just leave, slowly and deliberately.

Sasquatch do indeed use rocks and saplings as weapons, however. I found the following in an anthropology book, chapter one, page one.

It is the edge of an Etruscan plate, which dates it from 800 BC to 300 AD. It has been written that Sasquatch were employed by some armies as warriors. The "great ape" depicted is holding a sapling and throwing a rock. Yes, if they are indeed a people, they can be soldiers just like us.

Keep in mind that, in the forest, you are in their habitat. You are in their home. If they don't know you, especially, they will be wary of you and your actions. They will know you are there long, long before you are aware of their presence. Never think you will sneak up on a Sasquatch.

Which brings us to trust.

Chapter 4: Establishing Trust

I made mention that Pamela and I lived in a small cabin deep and isolated in the woods. We rented this cabin for three years, and with the exception of winters (we might be nuts, but we're not crazy) we were there.

Looking back, this is generally how it went down...

Year One: We had interactions close to the cabin, but not too close. Tree knocks, coyote mimicry and the like from a safe distance. Our Sasquatch tested us to observe what we would do, which wasn't much because we didn't understand what we were dealing with. I recorded some of it, such as the coyote mimicry (according to Native Americans), which can be listened to on YouTube. Just google "Sasquatch vocalization Dave Gibson" and you'll find it, or if you're on Kindle, click the link- https://www.youtube.com/watch?v=69IuQ4-rAec

Looking back through my blog, in 2013 I made a passing reference to Bigfoot possibly being about, but that was meant to be tongue-in-cheek humorous since I did not believe Sasquatch existed. I thought there might be a slight chance such a cryptid might exist in the Pacific Northwest, but I doubted it. Where is the proof? Where are the bodies?

Year Two: 2014 was a pivotal year for Pamela and me. Pivotal in that we both did an about face on the existence of Sasquatch. For us, it began when our Sasquatch left more obvious signs of his presence.

There was an extended drought that year. Area streams dried up, as did the one running by our cabin. We had the dogs in the car and were headed for our property a mile away for them to romp, when part way up the driveway Pam exclaimed "The tarp is off the well".

The well is dug and there is a concrete cistern in it. On top is particle board, and it is covered in a heavy blue tarp and tied on with a thick rope. I know this because I was down in there to replace the foot valve earlier that year.

The tarp was tossed off to the side. The rope was not untied, but broken. The only thing powerful enough to break a rope like that would be a bear, I reasoned.

As I was tying the tarp back on, Pam said "Come look at this!". She was pointing to the ground.

"What is it? A bear track?" I asked.

"No. Come look."

I walked over and looked at it. It looked like a barefoot human print, but short, and fat.

"That's too small to be a human foot print," I said.

"No, the heel is back here," she replied, as she pointed to a spot way behind the stick.

This was to be the first of many footprints that we would find, despite our very rocky ground and heavy leaf clutter.

I know it is hard to see in print, but the toes are at one end of the stick at around 1 o'clock (for all you kids who grew up with digital clocks, ask your grandfather) and the heel is where Pam is pointing. In a high resolution photo, you can see toes and the mid-tarsal break. In Jeff Meldrum's book *Sasquatch: Legend Meets Science* he describes the mid-tarsal break. In layman's terms (me) a mid-tarsal break is an added joint at approximately halfway on the foot to facilitate walking. Apes have mid-tarsal breaks.

Wait, you're thinking. I thought you said Sasquatch aren't apes? Yes I did. Not in the Mountain Gorilla sense. But they are also not human. They are somewhere in between. A mid-tarsal break just makes sense for an eighteen inch foot, like this one.

Later that year, I found evidence that totally sealed the deal for me that Sasquatch is real. A hand print.

The little town we lived in has 38,000 acres, mostly forested, and only 550 people live there. There are many dirt roads. One, in particular, I liked driving. Being such a dry summer, the road kicked up a lot of dust behind our Kia Sorento, which curled up and covered the back of the car in dust. I didn't care though. We treat this poor Kia like a farm truck anyway.

I got to the cabin, loaded the dogs into the back of the car, and took them to the property to run. Later, I loaded them back in and returned to the cabin. Upon opening the hatch to let them out, there it was. A huge hand print.

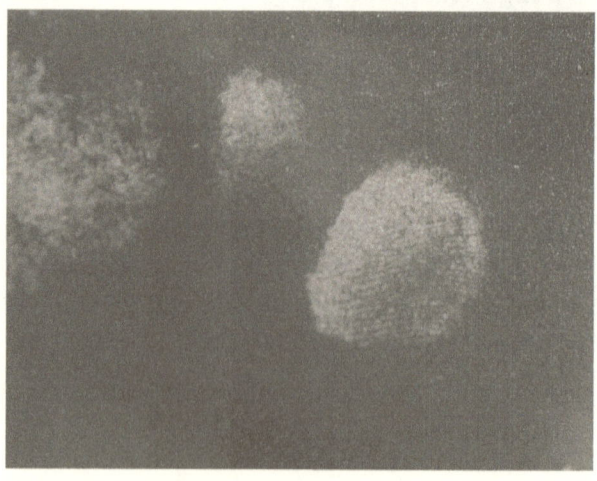

This was baffling. It was obviously a hand print. A huge hand print. But what are those lines at the base of the palm and towards the thumb? It looked like corduroy.

I won't rehash the whole tale since it is already told in my book *Living Among Sasquatch: A Primer*, but the corduroy-like lines are friction skin, something apes have to aid in grasping heavy objects. Note the lack of whorls in the fingerprints. I don't know if all Sasquatch fingerprints lack whorls, but ours did.

This was the most difficult evidence to confirm as Sasquatch. It was finally a forensic anthropologist in San Francisco who had other prints to compare it to, who confirmed it was a match to his.

Hand prints are extremely rare, I found out, and chances are that you will never find a clear hand print. But watch your car windows anyway.

Now, convinced we had a large monster stalking our cabin, what do we do? Like any red blooded American, I turned to the internet. Being an ex-computer systems designer, I tend to study things to death, much to the dismay of Pamela and my so-called friends. From the internet, I quickly learned that Sasquatch is a horrible monster that will kill you and eat your dogs too. It's on the internet so it must be true, right?

I also learned that just about every Native American tribe has legends of Sasquatch. Well, there is an Iroquois Museum not far from the cabin in Howe's Cave, New York so we needed to go there and talk to them about it.

The Iroquois Indian Museum is a delightful place and we both enjoyed it. As we were leaving and Pam was buying a necklace from an Iroquois couple minding the store, and me being me, I took the opportunity to ask the man if he had heard any stories of Sasquatch and the Iroquois. He smiled slyly and didn't say much, other than that he had heard some stories as a boy. But next to him, the woman's face lit up, and Pam and she had a very animated conversation about Sasquatch. She said that the Iroquois refer to them as the Keepers of the Forest who watch over everything that happens there.

Being hard of hearing, I wandered away to let Pamela and the Iroquois woman jabber away. On the ride home, I asked Pamela what the woman said.

"So is it going to kill us?" I asked.

"No," said Pamela. "If it wanted to, it would have done so by now. It likes us, and knows we have good hearts."

Well, that was a little bit reassuring.

"What about our dogs and cats?" I asked.

"The woman said to just tell the Sasquatch that we love our pets and ask it not to harm them," she replied.

"What? That has to be the dumbest thing I ever heard! What does she mean by that?"

Pamela just smiled. When we got to the cabin, she walked to the wood line and said in a clear voice "Please don't hurt out dogs and cats. We love our pets."

And then she walked into the cabin. Alrighty then. But long story short, in the three years there, we didn't lose any of our dogs and cats. We did lose one kitten, but that could have been to an owl or hawk. I also noticed that all predators vanished. No more bears, coyotes, foxes, or anything else that might harm our pets were to be seen anywhere near.

Year three: This was our final year in the cabin, and a memorable one, especially for Pamela. This was a Facebook post that Pamela made. I copied it and inserted it word for word in my first book, and now again in this book. I think no one can describe a sighting better than the person who saw the Sasquatch. This is in Pamela's own words...

Tuesday, May 5, 2015;

HOLY EFFIN CRAP!!! Ok, the sun is coming up and in FL that doesn't happen until about 7am in the spring. So I'm up with the sun.... But it's only 5:30. I get up and both Ruby and Olivia want out for morning potty. Well I know Olivia is going to go running and barking so I stick her on a leash to keep her from doing that and let Ruby out while walking Olivia. I figure I might as well look for footprints since it's so early. What do I find? Another handprint on our car!!! A bigfoot handprint! Only it's much smaller than the one from last year. And it's fresh! Like morning dew in the air fresh! Holy crap... Dogs inside! My heart is racing. Do I wake up David? It's 5:30. He never gets up before 9. Too bad, I have to tell him, so I run upstairs and frantically tell him there's a handprint. He groggily says take a picture.... So I run back downstairs, grab his camera and go creeping outside. I have my back to the wooded pines and briars near the car and try to get a good angle for the photo. I clicked one shot, two shots... The hair on the back of my neck prickles and then heavy thudding footfalls are behind me! Holy crap! What the hell is that??? My brain screams bigfoot! Run! So I ran back in the cabin and up the stairs again. My heart is pounding out of my chest and I'm shaking from head to toe! "David! David! Get up! I had an underwear changing moment! He's out there! I heard him!" So now poor David is up, not awake and pulling on his jeans and tee shirt. I open the door to go back out and Leo the cat comes racing in with a scared look and bounds straight up the stairway never slowing down. I'm standing inside the screen door on our little porch waiting for David and just looking and listening when a black shrouded head drops from view behind a small stand of pines not more than twenty yards in front of me! Now I'm whisper-yelling "I saw it! Right there!" Pointing to the stand of trees. David goes strolling out yelling at it that he's pissed and it needs to come here right now! I told him not to piss it off or it might smack him with a tree again.... So now, with reenforcements behind me, I wander up the driveway a little looking for footprints. Nothing.... Rats. Dave goes back to the car and we examine the handprint more closely. Much smaller than the one from last year. I said "uh oh.... David, if this is a young one, that means there's a mamma around somewhere. We all know how mamma anything can be if it feels it's young is in danger." Ugggh.... Now we will need to be extra vigilant about the dogs. Hopefully the bigfoot family are good hunters and catch wild prey regularly or else my pets are going to be their dinner.

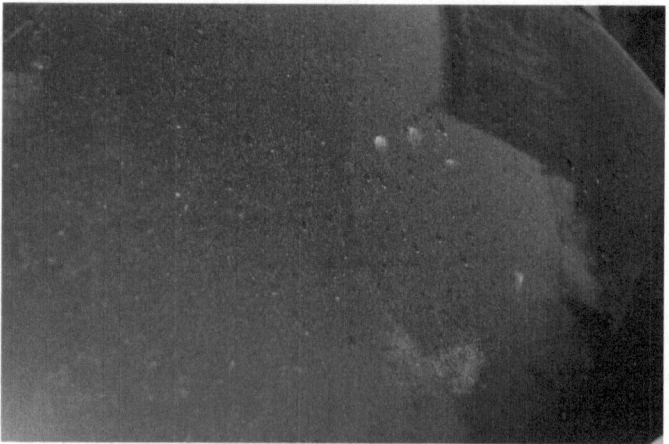

That, my friend, is typical Sasquatch behavior. Despite sighting reports to the contrary, I firmly believe that you will not see a Sasquatch unless it allows you to, either because he likes you, or just doesn't care if you do. I think Pamela's buddy was so excited that we were back that he announced his presence by running behind her, and then stood a few dozen feet away to allow her to see him.

Are Sasquatch shy and elusive? Yes they are. It took two years of almost daily interaction between Pamela her buddy to get to the point where he let her see him for a few fleeting seconds, and then she never saw him for the rest of our time there. Sad, but them's the facts. Which is why when I read a posting on Facebook wherein someone says they see Sasquatch often, I simply shake my head. And television programs where "researchers" go out in the forest and whoop and holler? Nonsense. You might get a whoop response if you're really good at it, but you won't find Bigfoot that way.

Establishing a trusting relationship with a Sasquatch is imperative to interacting with him. Interactions that create a sense of trust and security between you means a possible sighting, and communicating, which is the next chapter.

Chapter 5: Communication

So at this point, probably at least half of you are shaking your heads while reading this book.

"C'mon Dave... Sasquatch will kill your dogs and eat your children. Everyone knows that. Just pick up any Sasquatch book and that's what it will tell you. Why in the world would you think Sasquatch is your forest buddy? What proof do you have that they aren't anything other than an undiscovered North American ape?"

I'm glad you asked, because that is what I thought too when I first got into this whole Sasquatch thing. Sasquatch were to be feared, according to everything I read. What changed my thinking was their ability to communicate.

But let me add first that the only thing that would be considered proof of the existence of any cryptid is a body. Nothing else will do. No video, no audio, no DNA, no photographs, no eyewitness testimony, no casts of footprints. Those are all bits of evidence, and like a CSI piecing together evidence from a crime scene to arrive at a theory, that is all researchers are doing. Collecting evidence. Some better than others, for sure, but it is only evidence, including what follows.

Now, I can't take credit for suspecting Sasquatch may be of Asian origin. Ron Morehead and Al Berry recorded the famous "Sierra Sounds", among other vocalizations, between 1972 and 1975. The vocalizations recorded were described as "Samurai chatter", a very fast and staccato-like language similar to Chinese.

Linguist expert R. Scott Nelson has analyzed these recordings and concluded that it is indeed a language, spoken twice as fast as known human languages. Nelson claims that to follow Sasquatch dialogue, recordings must be slowed to half speed to be transcribed. Thanks to his military training as a linguist, Nelson was able to create a Sasquatch alphabet. Grammar and translations are not known at this point and may never be without a Sasquatch to interpret for us.

Pamela came to me one morning and said she heard a group of Sasquatch talking to each other as they passed by our cabin in the middle of the night. She described it as monkey chatter. I googled and played Berry's and Morehead's Samurai chatter for her and she said "That's it!". So we have a possible match between Sasquatch in the Sierra Nevada Mountains of California and the Adirondack Mountains of upstate New York.

Later, while trying to understand glyphs, I was at the same time re-reading Dr. Jeff Meldrum's *Sasquatch: Legend Meets Science*. Meldrum postulated that our Sasquatch may be a descendant of Gigantopithecus Blacki, a very large Asian ape that may have crossed the land bridge across the Bering Sea to North America that melted and disappeared 12,000 years ago.

Hmmm... Samurai chatter... Asian ape... could glyphs be Asian writing?

It was October 11, 2015 when I connected these dots.

Pam and I had been finding odd groupings of sticks around the cabin. One that was common, in particular, vaguely resembled the letter A. Pam thought that perhaps it was our Sasquatch's signature. His sign. I wasn't convinced. Just piles of sticks, I thought. But then Pamela noticed this one outside our cabin window, in plain view. It was an A, but probably knocked slightly askew by our dogs who used that path to run to the woods.

OK, I thought. This is getting freaky. I wonder if it is a signature... or perhaps more?

Pamela loves dragonflies, so she left her own signature on the stump by the cabin. This is what she left...

Her signature is supposed to be a dragonfly of sorts. If you look really closely, you can also see a dragonfly earring she left (it may not show up in print, but you can see these photos in a public album on facebook. Look me up- www.facebook.com/dave.gibson.7355).

Last night, she went out to check the stump. She came running back to the cabin. I was inside on my laptop, no doubt again saving the world on Facebook with my pithy remarks, when she came running by the cabin window wall. I immediately sprang into action and looked to see if she was being chased by anything. Nope. But she came flying into the cabin....

"David! Come and see this!!"

"OK. Should I bring my camera?"

"YES!" she exclaimed as she ran back out the door.

So I did. What I found was this.

The dragonfly earring remained, but the sticks were rearranged, and one added to the left leg.

I decided to review Chinese symbols. I found this page - http://www.zein.se/patrick/3000char.html (note- new browsers from Chrome and Edge have eliminated manual encoding and now improperly autodetect encoding and the Chinese symbols may not display as they should at that link. If you can, set the encoding to GB2312).

If you look at number six, you'll see that the inverted V shape means "man".

Scroll down to number 13. The letter "A" shape with a horizontal line means "big", as in a man with outstretched arms (the one that got away was this big!).

Huh. See the little twig placed on the left leg of the A in the photo above? Yep. Now scroll down to number 197. That means "great".

You've now got it. Great big man. OK then. We're dealing with a creature who can speak a language, read, and write with sticks.

"But Dave," you're still thinking, "that's not bad, but I'm not convinced. Show me something pursuasive."

OK. Pamela was starting to buy into my theory that Sasquatch are Asian in origin and although there is no doubt that their language may have evolved over time, as has our own, the basics must still be there. She asked me for the Chinese symbol for "friend", which is as follows...

I sketched out the symbol and handed it to Pamela, who ran out to her stump and made the character with sticks.

The next day, she ran into the cabin again all excited. The Sasquatch did not rearrange her sticks, but removed the thick sticks that made the lower horizontal line and X and replaced them with skinny ones, as the below photo shows.

I guess Sasquatch are sticklers for proper spelling and corrected her.

After posting stick glyphs and my ideas about translating them on Facebook Sasquatch groups, the people who weren't sure I was off my nut started messaging me with photos of glyphs. Many were just piles of sticks with no meaning, but others were obviously made by an intelligent being.

One, in particular, intrigued me. I pulled up the 3000 character Chinese symbol site and began scanning. I eventually had a match, so I messaged the sender.

"Was there any signs of a conflict in the area?" I asked.

"Yes, there was. Which is why I sent that photo of the glyph. What does it mean?" she replied.

"That glyph means there was a fight or a battle nearby. It is a warning," I answered.

Now, can I translate all of the glyphs I'm sent? No. Only about half. But that isn't surprising since a) I don't speak or read Chinese, and b) languages morph over time. There is no reason to think a Sasquatch language would be any different.

Are those the only ways Sasquatch communicate? Verbally and writing glyphs? No. There is gifting.

Chapter 6: Gifting

Gifting can be a controversial topic in the Sasquatch community, especially the gifting of food. Many, who believe Sasquatch to be an animal, claim that Sasquatch will become dependent on your food offerings and the day you stop feeding them is the day they become angry and aggressive. Not in my experience. Not the way we approached it.

Pam and I left food gifts for our Sasquatch. Nothing extravagant, and certainly nothing they wouldn't find locally. We did not leave candy bars, peanut butter sandwiches, pineapple, and so on. We only left things they would find in the area and eat anyway.

Well, in the interest of being honest, when I first got into all this and I too believed Sasquatch was an ape, I left it a banana on the roof of my car, out of reach of most forest critters. The next morning, the banana was still there, untouched. There was a single fingerprint on my car's back window. I didn't know, at the time, what that meant.

Now I know. The fingerprint was a Sasquatch acknowledging that he was there. He had no idea what a banana was and had no intention of eating it. I also now know how stupid I can be sometimes.

Pamela left our Sasquatch an apple on the stump. It was ignored.

Pamela got more elaborate and tried leaving a cattail as a food offering, along with her dragonfly signature and a tiny A glyph.

The next day, this is how she found it.

The small A glyph that Pamela made was gone, replaced with a larger A made from Pamela's dragonfly, and the cattail was placed on top of it, giving it back to Pamela.

I pondered this for awhile, and later related one of my favorite Sasquatch stories to Pamela.

If I remember correctly, this happened in the 1930s, but the date isn't really important. A young boy was walking barefoot down a dirt road, heading home. In each hand was a dead chicken. Suddenly, a giant Sasquatch stepped out of the woods and approached the boy, who was frozen in fear. The Sasquatch said nothing, but pointed to the chickens. The boy nervously handed the two chickens to the Sasquatch. The Sasquatch handed one back to the boy, turned, and walked back into the forest.

I think Sasquatch share, I told Pamela. They won't take anything if there is only one. Sharing is how they all survive. Try cutting the apple in half and leave both halves, I said. See what happens.

Just before we left to go camping, she cut an apple in half and left both halves on the stump. When we returned to the cabin a couple of days later the dragonfly earring and an apple half were on the part of the stump towards the cabin, meaning it was for Pamela. The other half of the apple was gone. The Sasquatch took it. If it was a forest animal, it would have taken both.

Gifting is not a one way street. Sasquatch will also gift back.

Pamela was going to work early one morning. She left the cabin to go to her car but came back in to get me.

"There's a half a squirrel by my car door," she announced.

I went out to look, camera in hand. It was the back half. The tail was completely flattened to the point that it looked like a bird feather where something very heavy stood on it. There was a hole where it's innards used to be. Part of it's spine was missing. It was pulled apart with great force, it seems. Maybe in repayment for the apple, the Sasquatch left Pam half a squirrel.

No, we didn't eat it. We secreted it to our property and stuck it on the bottom of the burn pile. We didn't want to insult our Sasquatch.

Our Sasquatch also left this on the stump, jammed into the shard that stuck up from being cut many years ago.

It was a half a leaf (Sasquatch share) with a frozen moth on it. The moth sort of resembles a dragonfly, I suppose. It was a food gift meant for Pamela.

Food is not all that Sasquatch gift. Not by a long shot.

I have a 1952 Ferguson TO-30 tractor on our property. I ride it a lot, using it for many tasks, from collecting rocks to skidding logs. I'm sure our Sasquatch watches with great interest and fascination.

One day, I was walking towards the game trail (why, I don't recall, but it isn't important). Laying on the ground were two bright blue bungee cords. I have bungee cords that stretch the tire chains on my tractor to keep them on. These must have fallen off, I figured. I went to my tractor and all cords were intact. Not wanting to appear ungracious, I added the two bungees to the tire chains.

Another time, I walked up to the tractor-trailer trailer that Pam and I use to store our stuff, including many tools, generators, furniture, and so on. The first thing I do when I arrive on our property is to unlock the trailer so I have quick access to needed tools and such. As I approached the steps, there, in a pile, was a bunch of washers, hose clamps, barrel nuts, and assorted other fasteners. Where could all this come from? We only have one neighbor, Earl, an 80 plus year old guy, and he would never do anything like this. Sasquatch? Did he watch me repairing something (tractor, generator, etc.) and understood that I used parts like this? Where would he get this from? The hunting preserve next door?

But the best happened to Pamela. She loves horses. She's had horses since she was three, and here in Florida now manages a horse ranch. She brought our friend Bill's horse, who was corralled at Earl's next door, over to our property to sit on our deck to get the snarls out of her mane. She wound up cutting off much of it, and she left the clippings laying on the ground for the birds and mice to nest with.

A few days later, she arrived at our property, parking in her customary spot. We are creatures of habit, I guess, and she parked exactly where she always did. I was already on our property puttering around. She was sitting on the deck, and I climbed down from the trailer to go sit with her. As I passed her car I noticed this sitting on the ground by her driver's door.

I picked it up, walked over, and handed it to her.

"What's this?" I asked.

Pamela examined it.

"It's Katy's mane, straightened and tied up in a bow."

Our Sasquatch understood Pamela's love of horses, and gave her a thoughtful gift. It is one of our most cherished Sasquatch keepsakes, and sits here on my desk in a baggie.

We and our Sasquatch have exchanged many little gifts. It is one of the most interesting facets of Sasquatch behavior to me. Gain their trust and friendship and they can be downright neighborly.

Chapter 7: What Did the Family in Honobia Do Wrong?

So far, I've described what I believe Sasquatch is. I discussed mindspeak and Honobia, which is the impetus to writing this little booklet. I've discussed aggression, establishing trust, communicating, and gifting. What did the Honobia family do wrong? Everything, at least according to my experiences.

As I mentioned previously, I understand the fear people have when first confronted by a cryptid so overpowering as a Sasquatch. I also understand the perceived need to grab a gun to defend your family. But also try to understand the behavior of Sasquatch.

Sasquatch are just trying to live. They are a people of the forest, and understand only the ways of the forest. Survival is number one on their Maslow's Hierarchy of Needs chart, with food being a top priority.

I suspect that Sasquatch share food with each other to survive. If one kills a deer, it is shared with all. Since both they and we are a people, they will not only share their food with you, but expect you will be a good neighbor and share your food with them. Deer meat left in a freezer in an open shed is you sharing your food with them.

Talk to them. Out loud, in English, as the Iroquois woman said we should do concerning our pets. I don't know how it works, or why it works, but it seems to. I doubt Sasquatch speak English, but they understand somehow. Can they sense our emotion and comprehend? Is it mindspeak? Coincidence? Did the family in Honobia ask the Sasquatch to take what they need, and leave the rest? No. They started shooting.

Shooting at Sasquatch seems to be a very bad idea. They fully understand what a weapon is and that you are trying to harm them. Heck, even my female pit bull knows what a gun is and panicked when I once looked down the barrel of a revolver (yes, it was unloaded). Shoot at a Sasquatch and Sasquatch might retaliate, as in the following Ape Canyon incident.

You seasoned Sasquatch folk are no doubt aware of the problem that prospectors had at Ape Canyon in the state of Washington, which is near Mount St. Helen. But bear with me while I give a condensed version to those readers not familiar.

In 1924, prospectors staked out a claim and built a small cabin on it. It was made of logs chinked with mud, and with a metal roof. It had no windows, and only one door.

Strange sounds were heard in the area. The prospectors started carrying guns. One prospector was at a nearby creek when he saw an "apeman" watching him from the other bank. He shot at him. The "apeman" made good his escape, but that night the cabin was attacked by a large group of Sasquatch. They pelted the cabin with rocks, and tried to break down the door and beat in the roof. The prospectors fired through the door and roof. Eventually the attack subsided.

The next morning, the prospectors decided to hightail it out of there. On their way, they saw a Sasquatch watching them leave. A prospector shot him, killing him as he tumbled over a cliff. They left Ape Canyon and never returned.

Some believe this tale verbatim, in its entirety. Others think the prospectors may have concocted the story to keep claim jumpers away. While I don't know if it actually happened or not, I think it certainly could happen. If Sasquatch are indeed a people, as they have demonstrated to my wife and I, they will defend their friends and family, just like you would. Be very wary of making a threatening move of any kind towards a Sasquatch.

So what should you do if you do come face to face with one? No one really knows since this happens so rarely, and the face to face encounters you hear about are suspect, in my view. But this is what is done in my novels, and I think it is good advice if you find yourself in such an encounter.

Stand your ground, and make no sudden or threatening moves. Remain quiet (if possible). Extend your arms a bit with your palms open and facing up to show that you have no weapons. If you do have weapons, do NOT point them towards the Sasquatch. Give a small nod. Watch his reaction. My suspicion is that he will do the same, and then go on his way. If he in any way indicates that you should leave, you should do so. Back away, and then turn and walk slowly.

Let me be very clear on this. I am in a very small minority who think this way. Mainstream thinking is a Sasquatch is an animal and an apex predator who will just as soon kill you as look at you. But here is an amusing story for you to contemplate that refutes this.

I belonged to a Facebook group lead by a well known author and researcher, who will remain unnamed. He specializes in supposed nonfiction scary monster Sasquatch books. I tolerated his views because, well, I am a tolerant and respectful person. And remember that there are no experts, including me, so I considered his opinions.

Unnamed researcher/author made numerous statements that Sasquatch are violent apex predators. I disagreed, and he got quite agitated, probably because I questioned him on his own website. I pointed out that he claimed to have had two personal encounters with Sasquatch himself, one of them included coming face to face with two huge mean creatures. He ran for his life, yet here he was to talk about it. They didn't kill him. They didn't bluff charge him. They didn't even chase him. If this encounter indeed happened, which I question, it would be more like "Hey kid, get off my lawn!".

He tossed my questioning butt out of his group. Hey, I've been kicked out of worse groups than that for asking too many questions.

Chapter 8: How to Find Bigfoot

This one is easy. You don't.

What, you're thinking? But the book title says...

Yep. Let me explain.

Pamela and I never went searching for Sasquatch. Oh sure, we tramped through the woods looking for evidence such as tree bends and branch twists, but we never expected to sight any Sasquatch.

Sasquatch found us. That is what they do, their modus operandi if you will. Our Sasquatch began interacting with us from a safe distance with tree knocks and animal mimicry. He then got bolder and closer. He interacted with us (in particular Pamela) through gifts. And then finally, he showed himself to Pamela at the beginning of year three in the cabin.

Well fine, you're thinking, but I don't live in a cabin in the woods. What do I do?

Habituators, those who live where Sasquatch live, definitely have an unfair advantage here. Habituators have (or in our case, had, since we moved) almost daily interactions, and our Sasquatch quickly learn whether we have good hearts or black hearts, good intentions or nefarious ones. Compare the experiences between Pamela and me, and the family from Honobia. Two different approaches to interaction, and two different outcomes.

I have a plaque purchased from the old *Latitudes & Attitudes* magazine; "Attitude. The difference between an ordeal and an adventure".

So what do you do if you don't live where Sasquatch do? The next best thing. Become a weekend camper. Research and explore desolate areas with good public access to forest, water, and game (deer in particular). Make sure the area chosen has no humans living too close, and certainly no hiking trails. Search for tree bends pinned on the ends by logs or rocks, as opposed to natural tree bends. Look for twisted tree branches since only a hand with a thumb can twist a branch. If you find evidence, and it appears somewhat fresh, you've found your area.

Now, camp. Pitch your tent, build your fire, set up your eating area, and have a good time. That's basically it, besides keeping your eyes and ears open.

Do not put up any game cameras. From my experience and those of serious researchers, cameras are Sasquatch repellent. There are many theories as to why this is, but no one really knows. Some say the Sasquatch can sense infrared, others suspect they can hear electronics, and others say that Sasquatch see them in the forest and know they don't belong. Many Native Americans believe Sasquatch are clairvoyant. But what I know is that when I put up a game camera, our Sasquatch vanished. He was gone for several weeks, even though I took the camera down. I violated his trust. He was miffed.

If you leave a camera up, you may return to find it smashed to bits as two researchers from Ohio told us happened to them.

If you bring a gun, keep it hidden. Keep rifles in your tent or vehicle. Keep hand guns out of sight, at least in a holster that conceals most of the weapon.

Just go about your normal camping business. Go hiking, fishing, or whatever you enjoy doing. Sasquatch are very curious. It is entertainment for them, something outside of the norm. If you're in the right spot, they'll quickly find you.

The key, though, is that to have close and frequent interactions, you have to earn their trust, and you do that by going to the same camping spot as often as you possibly can. If you aren't ready or able to do that, you won't earn their trust, at least not as quickly, and you may get frustrated and give up.

You can experiment by leaving food. As previously discussed, leave food they would find in the area naturally. Leave at least two of each food item.

Do not leave trash behind. We had a garbage can on our property. Pamela grilled hamburgers one evening and tossed the baggie that the raw hamburger was in into the garbage can. The next day I noticed that the garbage can was moved and a Sasquatch neatly removed the baggie, and bit the baggie in two to get at the leftover raw meat.

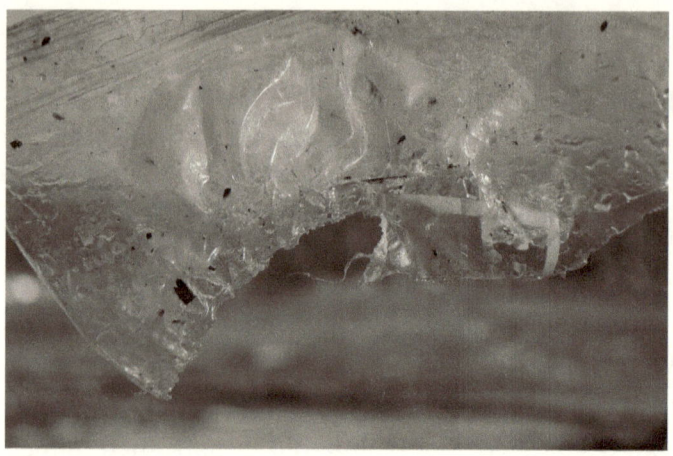

I never found the other half of the baggie. I hope our buddy spit out the plastic after chewing the hamburger up real good.

If you bring a dog with you, as silly as it sounds, announce that your dog is your pet, and to please not harm it. I know, I know... just do it when your friends aren't looking.

And watch your dog(s) closely. Their senses of smell, hearing, and eyesight are much better than ours. You dog will sense a Sasquatch long before you will. He may bark towards the woods, or he may run and hide in your tent depending on the dog.

When our Sasquatch was mimicking a coyote outside the cabin in our first year there, only the mighty hunting German Shorthaired Pointer was brave enough to venture outside of the cabin to bark at it. But this fearless hunting dog would not enter the woods and

instead stayed just outside of the cabin. My mighty pit bulls?
Dogs universally feared? Dogs bred to bring down livestock
much larger than them?   The male was curled up on the couch
and shaking, and the overly-protective female was hiding under a
table.

But by year three, our dogs were always outside. Almost
everyday they would start barking and run off into the woods,
only to return sometime later to lounge around again. I have a
hunch that they made friends with our buddy, who enjoyed the
dogs as we do.

The Pointer, by the way, began running throughout the woods.
She would leave in the morning and not return until late
afternoon. A hunting preserve a half a mile away has her on one
of its game cameras. I worried about her at first, since the
Adirondacks are home to many predators, but she was being
protected, I think. No harm ever came to her.

Leave the campsite as you found it. Leave no trace that you were
there with the possible exception of a circle of rocks that
contained your campfire. Show respect for the forest, and the
Keepers of the Forest will respect you for it. It is their home.

My best of luck to you in your search for America's most elusive
creature. I hope this booklet will be a help to you. If you've had
any success, contact me on Facebook and let me know. I'd enjoy
hearing your report.

Epilogue: We Are All Free to Believe What We Will

I hope you enjoyed this little book. Even if you disagree with my Sasquatch beliefs, which you are of course free to do, since just about everything about Sasquatch is a theory based on collected evidence. But in the case of us habituators, theories are also based on observation of Sasquatch behavior, and their reactions to things we do. If you're in disagreement, I hope I've perhaps opened your mind to what is possible. We will never know the truth until another Dian Fossey comes along and earns their trust completely and observes Sasquatch for an extended period by living among them.

Authors live on reviews. It is how we get the word out to others. While my books are available from many outlets, from Amazon to Barnes and Noble to Lulu to your corner bookstore, Amazon is the go to place for reviews. On a scale of one to five, if you enjoyed this book, I'd appreciate a four or five star review. If you did not enjoy it, it is not possible to leave a review. ;)

Finally, I will leave you with an excerpt from my last novel *Weak in Body, Strong in Mind and Spirit* that deals with the issue of beliefs.

In my fictional world of Sasquatch, they live in tribes and are guided by a Circle of Elders, the oldest and wisest of each tribe. Pamela is my real life wife, of course, placed in a fictional setting. Actually, all Little People (humans) in this book are real life friends, with the exception of the child molester.

Windago and Aurora are Elders, Aurora being a very ancient female, about 340 years old. Keizer is the mother of a little Sasquatch named Ady, who has a prominent role in the book and is a real hoot as she readily accepts her new found Little People friends. Love is natural, hate is learned, Sasquatch say.

I struggled with how to have Little People and Forest People communicate in the story, since our languages would be different. Finally, taking a cue from the Iroquois woman who told us to ask our Sasquatch to not harm our pets, and since it seemed to have worked somehow, I decided to use mindspeak. In my novels, mindspeak isn't spoken words, but a transference of thoughts, and enables Pamela, and others who have established a strong emotional tie with them, to converse with Sasquatch.

#

"You have arisen very early for a Little Person," said Windago.

"Yes, I can't sleep," said Pamela.

"Is something troubling you?" asked Windago.

"Yes," said Pamela. "Where did you come from?"

"We've always been here in the Ratirontaks," said Windago, "for as long as I can remember."

"No, that's not what I mean," said Pamela. "Where did we all come from? From very ancient times. Humans... Little People... have different ideas of where we came from. Some believe that we evolved from creatures in the sea. Our ancestors evolved over eons to become apes, and we evolved from apes. Others believe God... the Earth Mother, simply created us, and here we are. But where did you come from?"

"You ask very deep questions," said Windago.

"Let me," said Aurora. "Pamela, why do you ask such a thing?"

"Well," began Pamela, "we were talking to Keizer last night, and one thing that she said that struck me was that despite how very different we are, in so many ways, we are also much the same. That got me thinking about evolution and creation. Did Little People and Forest People have a common ancestor?"

"Pamela, those are questions that have no answers," said Aurora.

"I understand, but what do you believe?" asked Pamela. "How did the People of the Forest come to be?"

"Let me ask you first," said Aurora, "what do you think?"

"Well, I don't know what to think," said Pamela. "David is the nerdy researcher, and he's delved into this."

The Elders looked confused.

"Oh, nerdy researcher. Um... it means David spends way too much time trying to learn about things," said Pamela. "He has an unusual desire to learn things. Often things that aren't important to anyone but him."

"Is that bad?" asked Aurora.

"Well, no, but it can be annoying," said Pamela.

"How so?" asked Aurora.

"He spends countless hours reading books and internet sites to learn things. Some are factual, and some are just opinions of facts," said Pamela.

"So he is inquisitive and that is bad?" asked Aurora, without asking what the internet is.

"No, but then regaling me with it can be!" said Pamela. "Take Sasquatch... the Forest People. David says you might be large apes that traveled here from Asia over a land bridge, descendants of an ape called Gigantopithecus Blacki. Another theory is that we, Little People and Forest People, have common ancestors, but our evolutionary tree branched. We went one way and you went another."

"I see," said Aurora. "And this is important to you?"

"Yes. Well no, but yes," stammered Pamela. "What do you believe?"

"What do we believe?" said Aurora with a smile. "Well, we are all free to believe what we will. I will tell you what I believe..."

"Yes?" said Pamela.

"I believe that it doesn't matter."

"What?" asked Pamela, somewhat confused.

"Pamela," said Aurora kindly, "the People of the Forest live in the here and now. Yes, we have stories and legends of the past that we share to teach us how we should live today. We have Elders to guide our future. But we live for now."

"I'm not sure I'm understanding," said Pamela.

"Well, when you were confronted by the Bear yesterday, what were you thinking?" asked Aurora.

"I was thinking 'holy shit! What do I do?'" she answered.

"Yes. Did you ponder the origins of the Bear?" Aurora asked

Pamela smiled. "I see where you're going with this. No, I did not. I wondered about how to survive."

"That is how I feel, and how I think most Forest People feel," said Aurora.

"I know what you're saying," said Pamela, "but we have questions that need answers."

"No," said Aurora, "You have questions that want answers. Questions that you will never have answers to."

"I understand," said Pamela. "Yes, you're right."

"Pamela, it is not wrong to ponder such things," said Aurora. "I feel it is good to ask questions about the world we live in. It is good for our soul, for our being, to seek truth. But understand that while it is good... no, expected... to ask questions, there are some that no one but the Earth Mother can answer."

#

Note from the Author:

If I have answered questions about Sasquatch behavior for you, that's great. If I have created questions in your mind, that is even better. Question everything.

Keep a good attitude. Attitude is, indeed, the difference between an ordeal and an adventure. My sense is that Sasquatch can determine one's intentions. If you have a good attitude towards Sasquatch, want to let them live in peace, but show a desire to form a trusting relationship with them, they will understand and might make it happen. If you do not have a good attitude, it may very well become an ordeal.

Honobia.

www.ingramcontent.com/pod-product-compliance
Lightning Source LLC
Chambersburg PA
CBHW050336290526
45785CB00006B/2523